DESTINATION FREEDOM

The Journey of Choosing Him

ALISHA D. JOHNSON

Scripture taken from the New King James Version®. Copyright © 1982 by Thomas Nelson. Used by permission. All rights reserved.

Scripture quotations marked NLT are taken from the *Holy Bible*, New Living Translation, copyright © 1996, 2004, 2015 by Tyndale House Foundation. Used by permission of Tyndale House Publishers, Inc., Carol Stream, Illinois 60188. All rights reserved.

Scripture quotations marked MSG are taken from *THE MESSAGE*, copyright © 1993, 2002, 2018 by Eugene H. Peterson. Used by permission of NavPress. All rights reserved. Represented by Tyndale House Publishers, Inc.

Cover designed by Nskvsky

Printed in the United States of America
First Printing: July 2022
The Scribe Tribe Publishing Group

THE SCRIBE TRIBE
PUBLISHING GROUP

ISBN-978-1-958436-06-6 (print)
ISBN – 978-1-958436-07-3 (ebook)

This book is dedicated to the memory of the late Dr. Charles W. Lee Jr. and First Lady Elease Lee.

Table of Contents

Acknowledgements

Where do I begin to say thank you?! When I sit back and think about it all, thank you does not seem good enough. I am beyond grateful for what God has done for me and giving me this opportunity to write this book to share some very vulnerable parts of me that He allowed me to share.

I do not like to call names because I don't want to forget anyone, however, there are some names that I have to mention. I would like to say thank you to my Pastor, Sam Hamstra, and my Anthem Church family. Thank you, Pastor Sam, for speaking to what God placed on the inside of me and sowing into a dream God gave me years ago.

Next, I would like to say thank you to Kristen R. Harris of The Scribe Tribe Publishing Group. When I met you, I did not know who you were, but I remember the prayer you prayed in my ear and this book has been birthed and published because "God didn't forget about me."

I would like to say thank you to my brother, Bishop Daniel W. Lee Sr. for believing in me. I love you. My brother John Ross, I love you.

To all my family, your support through all of this has been immeasurable; I love you all so very much.

Bishop Tavis Grant, you adopted me and when I called you to tell you the journey I was embarking on, you said, "Let's go! You have my support, 100%!" Thank you!

To Pastor Reginald Johnson Sr., thank you for your support and encouragement.

Listen, I have some AMAZING friends! I cannot name them all, because I am likely to miss someone, but please know I love you ALL very much!

To my amazing children, Charles, Railei, Rachael and Isaac, you all have my heart. Thank you for loving your mom.

Lastly, to every person who will pick up this book, thank you for reading my "joy story" of finding freedom and choosing Christ.

Introduction

I am the one who has always had a journal. However, when I was a kid, they were not called journals. Then they were diaries, and I had those too. Writing was not my favorite thing, but I found it easier to express my thoughts this way. So, imagine my surprise when the Lord gave me this book. When I started writing in my journals, they were my own personal letters to God. I started each journal entry with "Dear God," and it would just go from there. "Help me to see myself the way you see me" was a theme that was constant in my letters to God. I used to hear all the time that when I realized who God made me, I was going to be great. I write this first book of many as a declaration of finally seeing myself the way God sees me!

Listen, a person can tell you how great you are, how important you are to the kingdom, how beautiful you are, and the list goes on. But until you believe it for yourself, it's like words just falling on the ground. These are just some of the things that I would hear, and they would go through one ear and out the other because I did not believe in myself or the giftings that God had put inside of me.

When you don't believe in yourself and you don't know your value, it will cause you to settle in places and or relationships where you are not meant to be. Have you ever wondered why you stayed stuck for so long or why there hasn't been any progression? Could it be that you never consulted the Lord, or maybe you wanted it so badly that it felt like God, so you took the plunge. My journaling days were always, "God help me to love myself like you love me." When we don't love ourselves or see ourselves the way God sees us, then how do we expect to find happiness? Happiness does not come from people, places or things but in fact, it comes from God and within. You can't expect anyone else to know your value if you don't know your own value. God wants to establish you, and He wants you to see yourself through His eyes. Once you truly see yourself, you will be amazed.

The Lord gave me this book with two main ideas in mind. The first one is to share some parts of my own personal struggles. I wanted to be transparent, that's how you get free. You don't get it by covering up with the appearance that you have always gotten it right. I will be the first to tell you that I didn't and that I missed it on so many levels. However, the Bible declares, "And they have defeated by him by the blood of the Lamb and by their testimony..." (Revelation 12:11 NLT) So, I asked the Lord which parts of my life that He wanted me to share because I wanted to divulge the most impactful parts of my journey. I wanted to be relatable and honest.

The other objective is to help others. I want to see you free in every area of your life. My desire is to see you walk into your God-ordained purpose and to live a full and complete life. I want you to come out of self-doubt, pity, rejection, and your feelings of unworthiness. You are more than a conqueror through Jesus Christ. There is nothing that you have said or done that you cannot come back from. There is nothing that you have done that could ever make Jesus Christ take His love from you. Romans 8:35 (nlt), "Can anything ever separate us from Christ's Love. " This scripture in the Bible resonated with me through some very tough times so I want to share it with you. I think it's important that you know that once you have asked for forgiveness you must also forgive yourself. **"So now there is no condemnation for those who belong to Christ Jesus."** Roman 8:1 (NLT) The transition won't be easy, but the Lord reminded me in the process, and I want to remind you, that it's not about what you've lost but about what you gained.

You can't transition into your next place or season with the same mindset; you must change your thinking. Philippians 2:5 (kjv) "Let this mind be in you which was also in Christ Jesus." You won't even be able to transition into your next with the same people and old habits. Those painful cut offs are necessary because they were not meant to go with you to this next place. In reality, they may fall off all by themselves. Leaves fall off trees so that they can survive the winter. There are some people and some things that need to fall off just so you can survive.

If you are reading this, your testimony will be, "So glad I made it!" Are you ready? I am so elated to share pieces of my life with you in a very real way to help you become all that God has created you to be. We are on a journey to freedom! My prayer is that by the time you finish reading this book, you will find freedom from the very thing that has been holding you back and keeping you from moving forward. 2 Timothy 1:7 (kjv), " For God has not given us the spirit of fear; but of power and of love, and of a sound mind." Fear has kept you bound for too long! The Bible also says, "So if the Son sets you free, you are truly free." (John 8:36 NLT) This is my testimony of finally seeing myself the way God sees me!

In the Beginning

So, I am writing a book! This is major for me; I wasn't eloquent in my writing and I disliked school for so many other reasons. One of the main reasons I did not like it was because I did not learn like the other kids, and I was a slow learner. In my younger days, they wanted to label me and put me in slow classes, but my parents would not allow them to do that. Thus, I had to work harder than the other kids because I had a point to prove. English was not my favorite subject and the best part about writing papers was not writing them at all. However, if I am honest, the first time I heard these words "I can't" was in school. Every person that studied to teach was not called to that profession. I experienced a lot of teachers telling me that I did not measure up and so eventually it became a part of my thought pattern. I did not come from a home where my parents would talk down to me; I came from a home where my parents pushed me and encouraged me. So how did I end up with the feeling that "I can't" when the word of God says, "I can do all things through Christ that strengthens me." Of course, at the time I was not thinking about that; I was just wondering why they would say that to a child. I failed third and fourth grade which defined me throughout grammar school. Never let a temporary moment define who you are. Yes, it happened, but it is not who you are or who God created you to be. It's just a part of your story.

What does it mean to be or to feel unworthy? I looked up this definition and it means, "never deserving effort, attention or respect." I wasn't the prettiest girl in school and definitely not the skinniest girl. I was a chubby girl who wore glasses and a uniform. But not the uniform with the short skirt. My mom found the one with the longest skirt and styled my hair in pigtails. I was not the one that boys liked and was not the one who made friends easily. I've always compared myself to others, measuring who I was against what they had and what they looked like. Often I thought, "If I looked like that then maybe... or if I had this then maybe..." I remember wanting friends so badly in school that I would have to give them something just to be my friend. When I had nothing else to give, they were longer my friend. So as a child, not even fully realizing what I was doing, I set something in motion that would follow me into my adult years. Be careful what you allow because you are teaching others how to treat you. Never give permission, you are the boss of your own life so own it!

Unworthiness carries various characteristics. I researched them and I must say that I found myself in many of them.. Let's journey together and go deeper. The first one I identified with was being "critical of yourself." I was always very critical of myself. I criticized myself in everything I did. Fresh out of college, receiving my B.A. was one the proudest moments in my life. In my senior year of high school, I had a counselor that told me I could never go to a four-year college because I did not have the grades and I would never be anything. So, imagine my disappointment. I was so hurt that I went home in tears. Though that was intensely painful, my story did not end there. I tried lots of things before I actually got to the school where I would receive my degree. I was ecstatic when I was accepted into Columbia College. Since I love music and love to sing and I really had no solid idea on what I wanted to do, I landed on majoring in music. It was fun and I met a lot of people, but it was an epic failure. I didn't pass any of my music classes, so my journey at Columbia ended after the first semester.

Next, I decided to try hair school because I thought I wanted to do hair. It was fun when I initially started and it soon went downhill. The first thing that happened was that I got robbed one day on my way home from school. I was walking to the train and the peson just walked up to me and snached my necklace; I did not know whether to run or what so, I paused for a moment and collected myself and hurried home. The other issue was that they fought almost every day. I mean what was I learning?! Finally, I got to school one day, and the owner had taken all the money, left and the school closed. It was all just a bit too much. I remember the day that I had enough. I went to a pay phone and called my mom. With tears streaming down my face, I told her that I was getting on the train and coming home. I was confident that God had to have something better for me. At that moment, I stopped living in what the teacher told me in school and decided to trust God for myself. It was then that I made the decision to attend South Suburban College for a year and get my grades to a point where I could transfer to a four-year college and that's exactly what I did. After completing one year and being told I should do two years, I went on to Trinity Christian College. There I met some amazing teachers who were actually called to teach and made a huge impact on my life. They would later become friends and very near and dear to my heart. My college professors saw what others did not see. So many of them stand out and if I could talk about them all I would.

My major was business, and yes, I struggled! It was a very hard journey for me. Some days, I did not think I would make it to the finish line. I had a professor by the name of Dr. Mark Ward who taught several of my business classes. I was failing every test, but I was still showing up, putting forth the effort and turning in my assignments. One day Dr. Ward said to me, "Alisha, I see that you are doing the work, but somewhere you get confused and you are not fully understanding." He vowed to help me so that I could succeed. Can I just tell you that help is a powerful word. Never be afraid to ask for it, we all need it. On days when we tested, he allowed me to come to class early. He used that time to go over every test question with me so I would understand and it didn't stop there. When the test came back and I missed it, he would allow me to retake the test at home with an open book.

In college you don't find many teachers like that. So where one teacher told me I couldn't, God sent me several teachers that said I could. God always has a ram in the bush. Some may count you out, but as long as God counts you in, you are still counted. Failure is not the end; it is only the beginning. It only becomes the end if you give in to the process.

I graduated from Trinity in 1999 and I was the only African American to graduate that year. It was truly a proud moment in my life. Some time after graduation, I landed a job at Trinity as an admissions counselor, so I was doing great. Then it happened, I got pregnant! I had made it through high school and college without a pregnancy. *Wait, not the pastor's daughter, daddy's girl and the minister of music pregnant with no husband.* In my mind, I just wanted to go and hide. It may not seem like a big deal, but for me it was huge! I had such high hopes for my life. I had adamantly said no babies out of wedlock for me. I was waiting for my husband, but it did not happen that way for me. I probably cried the entire first month of my pregnancy. If I am completely honest, I went back and forth about having my baby. I just couldn't believe that I had gotten pregnant and I considered making it go away. It felt like everyone was talking about me, looking at me with shame when in reality I was my biggest critic. While I was busy looking down on myself, all God wanted me to do was repent and move forward.

I felt like my father was so disappointed in me that he would not love me anymore. Yet, I remember vividly the day he wanted to talk to me, and his words soothed my heart and eased my fears. "I have not lost one ounce of love for you, not one." The tears raced down my face, but it was in that moment that acceptance came, and I was no longer critical or ashamed of what I had done. The Bible declares that all have sinned and fallen short of the glory of God. I was not exempt from that part of scripture and neither are you. The thing that is keeping us from being connected and finding grace in what seems to be a hopeless situation is us. God made it possible for us to come boldly before the throne when he died for us. So, we just need to ask God for forgiveness and find Him in our situations because I promise you sis, He is right there. It was when I asked for forgiveness that I found peace and received the love that was waiting on me. Sis, I know that it happened, but God wants you to forgive yourself. He has so much in store for you. Romans 8:1 says, "There is therefore now no condemnation to those who are in Christ Jesus..." Forgive yourself for you have been forgiven and you no longer have to live in the guilt of your past.

Heavenly Father,

Help me not to be so critical of myself but help me to love myself and receive your forgiveness and forgive myself and move forward in your unconditional love for me. In Jesus' Name, Amen!

What Was I Thinking?

I hope you are still with me because we are still on a journey of diving deeper into how feelings of unworthiness manifest in our life. Another characteristic I found was being afraid of making wrong decisions. You may be wondering, how is this a trait for feeling unworthy? Have you ever reflected back on your life and thought, "I made some horrible decisions," or thought "Why did I do that? What was I thinking?" Let me tell you, this is a song I know all too well. I made some mistakes and yes, I stayed there for a while, but you don't have to stay there. You can recover and still have everything that God promised you. Sometimes we make bad decisions in the heat of the moment. Other times, when we feel our back is up against the wall, we make these decisions and we don't pray and seek God, when the word of God clearly tells us in Proverbs to acknowledge the Lord in all our ways and He will direct our paths. When we fail to acknowledge and pray, we tend to go down a path that was never meant for us, but God has to show us that He is truly the author of our lives.

I remember when I first heard that my father's cancer was back. I was devastated, but he had beat it before and so I just knew he would come through it again. Anyone that knows a little about me, knows that I was a daddy's girl to my heart. My father was a pastor and growing up as a PK as they used to call it was different. I was with my dad all the time. I would wake up early every Sunday morning with him. The highlight for me was him picking out his suits and then I would pick out his matching tie each week. This was our routine, and it brought me so much joy. Then I would go and get dressed so I would be ready when he was ready to leave. My dad was a fast driver, and no one wanted to ride with him except me. I figured he was not going to hurt himself and he loved me, so he was definitely not going to hurt me. When we would get mad at each other, it was like the world was coming to an end; I never wanted him to be upset with me. Since my father was very secretive, he did not want anyone to know he was sick the second time around. So, my mom respected his wishes and never really said anything. It was on a need-to-know basis. This even applied to me as I was only given limited details. So, not really knowing all the details in full, I prayed daily that God would heal my father. I could not imagine my dad not being here with me.

The Lord let me know what was going to happen through a vision and a dream and even then, I was prepared but not prepared. I had the vision first. I was going to my dad's church the first Sunday in November; they were celebrating my dad's birthday. He was not there, but they still celebrated him. I got to church early that afternoon, and I just remember coming in, putting my things down, greeting everyone and then looking to the front of the church to see a gray casket right in front of the pulpit. I looked and then I looked away and I looked again and it wasn't there anymore. At the time I did not know for sure what God was telling me. However later, I had a confirming dream. In my dream, I saw my father dressed in all white. He wasn't sick anymore, his face was clear, he was barefoot, and he had on a white robe. It woke me up out of my sleep, but I knew then my father was dying. There was nothing or no one that could have prepared me for that day, except God and He did that for me.

The day he died I could not get ready for church, not really knowing what was going on. I made my husband late for church because I could not find anything to wear. Did I mention that I was also pregnant with my third child, and I wasn't a little pregnant. I was a lot pregnant! and it was a cold day on the 28th of December in 2008. We finally got ourselves together and headed out the door to church. We walked in church, and everyone was standing around like they were waiting for me to get there. What I didn't know was that my mom had already called the church and gave them the news of my father's passing. They pulled my husband to the side and whispered in his ear and then they asked me to come upstairs and where I was told to sit down. No one wanted to give me that news. It was my husband who told me that my dad had transitioned. My heart was crushed, and I cried and cried and then I cried some more. My hero here on earth, my favorite guy, and my first friend, the one who spoiled me was no longer here with me anymore. How was I going to navigate life without my dad?

They tried to get me to the hospital to see him, so I could say goodbye. While en route, we got a flat tire, and it seemed like we would never get there. When we arrived, I slowly took that walk down the hallway and the closer I got, I saw the room door open and my mother waiting in the doorway. She said "Alisha, don't cry. He went so peacefully and he had a smile on his face." Her words were intended to comfort, but the fact was that he was still gone. I could not bring myself to go into the room and bid farewell to my hero. My mom and my husband got a chair and sat me outside his room and I looked at him from a distance. I watched as his lifeless body was whisked away. That was a very sad day for me.

Losing a parent is not easy, but God promises to never leave us or forsake us, and this holds true for you as well. God will always be with you. Losing my dad was difficult which caused me to make some poor decisions I was not so proud of. I was never a person who handled stress very well; I would shut down completely, or I would just go to sleep and not even deal with it and hope when I woke up that it would be over. Communication was not one of my best qualities. I will be honest and tell you that sometimes it worked and sometimes it did not work. While this was my way of coping, it was not the best way and yes, I knew better.

Well, this particular time it did not work, and I did something really stupid. Honestly, I wasn't really trying to hurt myself or even kill myself, I just wanted someone to see the pain that I was feeling, and so I did it. I took twelve Tylenol five-hundred milligrams and called the paramedics and told them so they could come and get me. When they arrived, I had my son in one arm and my daughter in the other. They removed my children from my arms and gave them to my husband, walked me out to the ambulance and immediately began to work on me. While in the ambulance I made a phone call to someone who is like a mother to me and told her what I'd done. She stopped what she was doing and came to the hospital, and she called my mom. When my mother arrived, she was very angry with me.

She immediately questioned, "Alisha, do you think your father would be happy with you right now"? I could not respond. My mother was so upset with me that night that she did not stay in the hospital with me. That night I went through so many different emotions, from coming down off the high of the pills to scratching and itching all over, but not one time did they ever have to pump my stomach. I stayed in the hospital the entire weekend, and while I was there the Lord sent a word to me. **"Being confident of this very thing, that he that who has begun a good work in you will complete it...."** It was at that moment that even though I made this crazy decision that could have harmed me and taken me out of here, I knew that God's hand was on my life and that I had purpose.

I know it may seem hard right now and I know it hurt you when they had to leave, but God's word is true when He says in I Peter 5:7, **"Casting all your care upon him; for he careth for you.** God cares for you, He sees you and wants the very best for you. Life throws us all kinds of obstacles and many ups and downs, but it is how we deal with them that will ultimately define us. Pray this prayer with me:

Heavenly Father,

Help me when life throws me a curve ball. Help me to communicate and make godly decisions that will bring glory to You and Your peace in my life. In Jesus' Name, Amen.

It's Just a Diagnosis,
It's Not the End

Insecurity is a beast. That is the only way I know how to describe this word. Insecurity has broken up homes, caused some to lose jobs, and even destroyed some friendships. Insecurity has also caused some to settle for less than God's best in every area of their lives. We will go deeper into this later, but I want to tell you how I felt after my oldest son was born. Parenting does not come with a manual, and if you are anything like me, you probably wish that it did. Although I wasn't super young, I was a first-time mommy. I did not know what I was doing, and I was so worried about being a good mom to my son. He would cry so much! I think bedtime was his favorite time to cry because he would do it for hours on end, so it seemed like.

After I had him, there was a lot I could not do, and I did not understand why it was like that. There were times he would be in the bassinet crying, and I couldn't pick him up because of the pain that I was in. My mom would always have him and sometimes have to pick him up and give him to me. I know that this may not seem like much but it was a big deal to me; after all, this was my first kid. I was the one that needed to build a bond with my kid. The pain ultimately got worse and worse. There were days that I could hardly walk, one knee was the size of two knees. My mother would carry my son in the house and then have to go back to the car to get me. She had to bring me some shoes and though I did not have a cane, she would be a support for me because I could hardly walk. This was a hard time. I just had a baby and I could hardly take care of him because I was sick, and no one could figure it out right away.

I went to the doctor several times and got all types of blood tests; however, they were coming back normal, but I was still very sick. Then my hair started to shed, and it got extremely thin and started coming out. I remember trying all kinds of styles from braids to sew-ins. The hairstyles were ok, but they made me feel a way about myself. It was extremely frustrating because I didn't know what was wrong with me. Finally, my doctor sent me to see a rheumatologist. I was like, a what? We were desperate to find out what was going on with me. The doctor took one look at me and pulled my hair and said, "She has lupus."

Systemic Lupus Erythematosus is the most common type of lupus. It is an autoimmune disease in which the immune system attacks its own tissue causing widespread inflammation and tissue damage in the affected organs. It can also affect the joints, skin, and many other areas of the body. Can you picture me in the doctor's office, reading a pamphlet and then reading that there is no cure?! What! I started to cry as I wondered what this horrific disease was going to do to me. My mom, of course, assured me that I would be okay. "Your aunt has lived with this for many years and she is doing good. You will be fine," she comforted me. While it was some assurance, it still was not sitting well with me.

The doctor then asked, "Do you have any kids?"

"Yes, I just had a baby boy."

"Good, because you can't have any more," he quickly responded.

It was all just a little too much. My mom was saying not to worry about it and then I had the doctor saying no more kids. He was crushing my dreams of getting married and getting pregnant again, all while my hair was falling out. I just felt horrible about myself, I was in so much pain and now they were telling me that I would have to take medicine for the rest of my life. So many questions began to riddle my mind. *Why did it happen to me? Why was I affected with this? Is this my life now?*

I remember losing a lot of weight and just not really wanting to be around a lot of people in the beginning because I never knew when I would have a flare up. I always knew when one was coming because it would start in my hands. Can I tell you a diagnosis is just that, a diagnosis? It does not have to be the end; it is all in how you look at it. Just like I remember the doctors telling me about this disease, I also remember the day God sent that disease packing.

I was at a service at my home church, and I remember my brother having an altar call. He asked me a question, "Do you want to be healed?" My response was yes, and he laid hands on me, and I believed that I was healed. When I returned to the doctor for my regular check up, he examined me thoroughly and said, "I see no signs of lupus." I was rejoicing and giving God praise for what He had done for me.

What do you believe and whose report will you believe? In the Message Bible, Isaiah 53:1 says, **"Who believes what we've heard and seen? Who would have thought God's saving power would look like this?"** The key to me being healed was believing. Is there anything too hard for God? Maybe you have received a diagnosis and maybe you feel hopeless. Perhaps you feel as though it is the end. I'll tell you this, believe again! Hope again! After losing my hair, I thought my hair would never come back, but God! Not only did it come back, but it came back better than before! I also had two amazing children after the doctor told me no. God had the final say so. Sis, acceptance of what the enemy has done is never an option. Get back up and get in this fight. There is so much work for you, and I will tell you like they told me—there are women waiting on the other side for you to tell your story. Pray this with me:

Heavenly Father,

Help me to believe again. Don't let me see the diagnosis, but let me hope in You. Father, Your word declares that by Your stripes I am healed. Father, I believe the report of the Lord, and I believe that You are my healer. In Jesus' Name, I pray Amen.

Boundaries

People pleasing, I think we have all done it once or twice. If you were anything like me, you wanted everyone to be happy, even if it meant you had to sacrifice yourself and your feelings hoping somewhere along the way it might work out. When you try to please others, you sometimes lose who you are in the process. I said yes so many times to things that I did not want to do just to keep the peace. I also said yes when people offered to help me, not consulting God, just accepting people at face value, but I learned some powerful lessons.

The first lesson I learned was to consult the Lord. We must pray about everything. The other lesson was not to take people at face value for they have motives that you know nothing about. While I was making sure everyone else was happy, I was miserable. I had to learn to set boundaries. We must learn when to say yes, when to say no and be consistent. God is not calling you to say yes to everything. Ask yourself if it is purposeful, is it positive or negative, and is it going to push me closer to my destiny. If the answers to some or all these questions are no, then it's okay to walk away. If you don't want to do it and you don't feel led to, don't do it. People will put you in a box and say all sorts of things to make you feel guilty about choosing yourself, but at some point, you must choose you. If you don't, you can't possibly be everything God created you to be because you are trying to be everything for everybody else. I am so sorry to disappoint you, you cannot have it both ways. You can't be hot and cold. The people you are trying to please will never be satisfied, so set your boundary and move on.

Your gifts and your calling will not allow you to be accepted by everyone. You won't even be able to hang out with everyone. When God wants to use you, sometimes it is a very lonely road. Not because you can't have friends, but you can't have the friends that everyone else has. You can't do what they do. The calling on your life requires you to be separate. We want to take everyone and be a part of the popular crowd, but perhaps that is not God's will for you. Maybe they just can't go. Trust God's plan and His timing for your life. Once you realize this, you have accepted your identity in Christ Jesus, and you move into acceptance.

A prayer that I have always prayed to God is, "Let Your will be done in my life, and not Your permissive will but Your perfect will." Am I saying that God has two wills? Yes, He absolutely does. His permissive will allows it to happen just so you can see that it's not what you really wanted. So yes, God will allow you to get the job, the relationship and anything else that we sometimes desperately beg Him for just so that He can show and tell us, "That's not what I had for you."

"For I know the plans that I have for you declares the Lord, "plans to prosper you and not to harm you, plans to give you

hope and a future." (Jeremiah 29:11) God knew us before the very foundation of this world and He knew what we would become while we were yet in our mother's womb. When our will lines up with His will, God will make even enemies be at peace with Him. (Proverbs 16:7) This step is called embracing who God created you to be, not worrying about who likes it and who doesn't like it or who will support you and who won't. The reality is that they won't anyway, so you might as well shine your light as big and bright as possible and be everything that God has called you to be.

I love this scripture in the Bible; it has helped me push through when I thought I could not go on further. I want you to insert your name when you say this scripture out loud, and watch what it does for you. I know what It did for me, and my prayer is that it does the same for you. Psalm 46:5: **"God is in the midst of her (Alisha). She (Alisha) shall not be moved; God shall help her (Alisha), just at the break of dawn."** This is literally how I have this scripture written down in my journal. I encourage you to do the same thing as it is amazing what the word of God does for us when we just learn to trust what it says. Then when we make it personal, it becomes a daily part of us.

Pray this prayer with me:

Heavenly Father,

You are all that matters. Your will for my life is what is most important. You are the one that I want to please daily by living the life that You have called me to live. In Jesus' Name, Amen.

God never promised that it would be easy; however, He did say that He would be with us every step of the way, and you can count on that! You got this sis! There is work to be done!

My Yes, Your Yes

Listen, I come from a family of preachers, and the female preachers we had in our family lived in California. And I was ok with them being the leading ladies; I had no intentions of following in my dad's footsteps. I wish you could see me laughing while writing this and shaking my head. I have always said that God has a sense of humor. He knows how to get you when you least expect it. I had always been told, prophetically, that I would preach, and my response always sounded something like, who, not me. My father was a stark baptist. I mean, no pants in the church, choir robes if you had on pants and no women preachers. My dad believed that women should not be in the pulpit except on special occasions, and even then he still didn't want it. I am laughing remembering this and anyone who knew him is laughing too. This was my dad for real, but he was a great preacher. However just because he was a great preacher, that did not mean I was called to that same thing.

I knew I was different as a kid, but not called to ministry different. I just thought, I'm a PK and that sets me apart. So, when I heard it the first time, I instantly thought, "nope, I'm not doing this." So I pretty much ignored it and ran from it. Preaching and prophesying was not something I wanted to do. My dad was a preacher, my brother is a bishop and I have cousins in California who are preachers and prophets. That's enough, we're good, or so I thought.

You can run but you can't hide. I'm sure you have read the story of Jonah. The first thing he did was run, and even before he got to the whale, the Bible says that he found a ship, paid and got on. The Bible says that God caused a great wind in which the ship was about to break when they found Jonah to be the cause because he was running from the Lord. Message: don't run! You wonder why things are not right. If it's not one thing, it's another. Trial after trial and it seems like you are always going through instead of coming out. What has God told you to do that you are not doing. What are you running from? Why are you running? You can run but you can't hide, just ask Jonah. It's better to be like Nike and just do it. Trust me, you will save yourself time and heartache if you just listen the first time around.

I hear the wheels turning in your head, and I hear you saying, "I don't feel like I have what it takes." I said the same thing! Even writing this book, outside of just waiting on God and His timing, I thought of every excuse of why I couldn't do it. The story is told in the book of Exodus, chapter 4 when God calls Moses and tells him to go and rescue his people. Moses says to God in verse 4, **"Please Lord, I am not a man of words..."** (eloquent, fluent) He goes on to say, **"...for I am slow of speech and tongue."** The Lord simply responds in the following verse and says, **"Who has made man's mouth? Or who makes the mute or the deaf, or the seeing** blind? **Is it not I, the Lord?"** He then tells Moses to go, **"even I will be with your mouth, and will teach you what to say."** All God is looking for is your "yes" and the rest He will handle. He just wants you to be obedient.

My daddy could sing and preach. I mean he just had it, and I couldn't do it like him. My brother can sing, preach and play all the instruments. I wasn't gifted like that. But God wasn't intending on me doing like them or being like them, all he wanted was my yes! So, after a few years–and yes, I said years, I finally accepted the call to preach the gospel. On January 18, 2015, I preached my first sermon and months later the Lord spoke and said I have called you to be a prophetess, but it would be years later before I would walk totally into this.

It is not about how you feel, how you feel about yourself or your capabilities but it's totally and completely about God and your yes. The point of this section in the book is not for you to accept your call to preach. This section is for you to give God your yes! God tells Jeremiah, **"Before I formed you in the womb, I knew you...(and approved of you as My chosen instrument)"** Then He tells him, **"Do not be afraid of them (or their hostile faces) for I am with you (always) to protect you and deliver you,"** says the Lord. You have been anointed for it, you just need to do it, and do it in the name of Jesus Christ. Insert your name in the scripture above and make it personal, God is talking to you.

Ok, God didn't call you to preach, but maybe He called you to write. Get your notebook and just write; it will flow. You say

He didn't call you to write, but maybe He called you to be a nurse. So, go to school, take the classes and do it to the glory of God. Sis, all I am trying to get you to do is get up and get to work! There is someone waiting on you to fulfill your purpose.

Let's pray:

Heavenly Father,

I give You my yes. Help me to be confident in the things that You have called me to do. Father, help me to live out my purpose. You have equipped me to do the assignment, now help me to complete the assignment. In Jesus' Name I pray, Amen.

Walk it out! I am praying for you!

Pain Equals Purpose

P ain is inevitable, we all will experience it. However, it's what you do in that painful place that determines how you will come out on the other side of it. Pain should not make you want to give up on the world, instead you should allow it to push you into purpose. There are some things that happen, such as death, that we can't do anything about because it's a part of life. Death is hard, but when you know Jesus, you know to die in Him is a gain. I am saying this now, but please know I did not always feel this way.

My mother was much like my father. She did not want us to know how sick she really was. My mother took a cruise in late 2015 and she had a great time. When she returned, she was under the weather. It didn't happen right away, it was a slow progression. She and I both thought it had something to do with the weather, well at least I did anyway. So, I did not make anything of it. God working behind the scenes had allowed us to transition back to Illinois after living in Indiana for a while, and I was glad because I did not realize my mother was going to need me.

My mother and I had rituals that were just for us that we would keep. Every New Year's Day, we would get up and go out to the mall, not to buy anything but just for the sake of being out that day. Then we would head to lunch.Before she had gotten ill, we started going to the nail shop together, followed by breakfast or lunch depending on the time of our appointment. It was something that we enjoyed doing together. To know my mother was to love her. She was, and is, the strongest woman I have ever known. My mother was the kind to help anyone in need and would never let anyone know that she was the one behind the scenes. She was an amazing woman.

She was a mother to many, but I was her only daughter. Did I mention earlier that I was spoiled? I loved being my mom's only daughter, I was her best friend and she was mine. I could talk about my mom forever because that's how great of a mom she was to my brothers and me. However, I didn't realize when we were going to get our nails done and having lunch that she was preparing me for what was to come. I remember one day we were driving in the car, probably going to lunch, and she said, "Alisha I am moving to a senior home, and I am going to leave you your dad's house." I just paused for a moment and looked. She saw the bewilderment on my face to which she let me know that she was serious. I don't think I had a response at that time.

After a while, my mom asked me to ride to the doctor with her to get a shot and. My mother never let me drive her around. Don't ask! (Again, I am laughing!) We walked into the doctor's office and we headed to the cancer patients area. She saw the worry and concern on my face and then assured me that she did not have cancer, but that she was just there for a Vitamin

B shot. I am sure that you can imagine the sigh that I released. So eventually, that became a part of our routine as well, then instead of going out to eat, I would go to the store for her. I started getting up early to call to find out what she wanted to eat and then I would go fix breakfast and just sit with her when my work allowed me too. This went on for a while, after all this was our routine.

Then it happened, my brother called me and said we have to take mommy to the hospital. Of course, she did not want to go. I rushed over to the house, and I had never seen my mom like that before, so I am sure that you can imagine my concern. It took some doing but we finally got her to go to the hospital. We were on shifts at the hospital. I took the morning, my oldest brother and my aunt would have the afternoons on lock, and my other brother always spent the night. I would see him when I arrived the next morning. This became our routine daily. We made sure that she was never by herself. After about three to four weeks, my mom was transferred to a rehab facility where she received great care, and again we kept our same routine. I went in early and accompanied her to physical therapy; she wanted me to see her progress. I was always there, and she was happy.

There was one Sunday that I did not make it. My mother stopped calling unless she really needed something. Oh, but that time she called because I did not show up, and she thought I left her there by herself. Boy, did she let me have it! Needless to say, I showed up the next day and she was still a bit upset but she was okay after a while.

In June, after about two months of the hospital and rehab, my mother came home. We were so excited! My mother stayed home for only a week before she would have to go back to the hospital. I am so grateful for my relationship with the Lord. My mother never actually told me what she was feeling. She may have shared it with my brothers and others, but with me. So, one day while driving I was talking to the Lord and asking him about my mom. I inquired as to what was really going on, and the Lord simply said to me, "She has a choice." My mother was tired and ready to go home and be with the Lord.

The hospital called and said that my mother was really sick. Soon after that call, my brother called and said that she had emergency surgery and that she was on a ventilator and in ICU. I did not know how I was going to walk in there and see her like that. As I walked in the room and I saw her like that, she saw the tears streaming down my face and she shook her head at me, telling me not to cry. Seeing her that way just hit me in a way I never imagined.

My family still kept our same routine; we went and sat with her. I had a friend at that time who worked at Northwestern Hospital who came to see her and prayed and sang. He told me to sing to her as well because my mom could hear me. So after that, everyday I would sing to her. The song the Lord gave me to sing to her was, "He Touched Me." I would sing the course of that song to her everyday without fail, and I would tell her, "Momma, God is making you whole whether on this side or the other." I was confident that she was being made whole.

I went to church the following Sunday and a word was given to me that said she would be alright that she was in the hands of the Lord. I was told me to read Psalms 91 to her. So, that following Monday I went to the hospital and pulled up my Bible app and read Psalms 91 to her. When I got to verse 16, "With long life I will satisfy him and show him my salvation," her eyes popped open. I hadn't seen her eyes open in a while; she was always sleeping. As they opened, I just smiled at her and I said, "Hey momma," and grabbed her hand. I was then asked by the nurse to leave the room so they could clean her up. I exited without thought because I was just so excited about her opening her eyes.

When I returned, she was sitting up for a brief moment. As I walked in, her eyes just followed me all over the room. The nursing staff laid her back down and I walked to her bed side and wiped her tears. She did not open her eyes anymore. Later, my brother called the family together because we had to make a decision about taking her off the machine. That was probably the hardest decision my brother had to make, and it broke his heart.

On July 1, 2016, we turned the machines off. She didn't go right away, but it took her about forty-five minutes, and she had transitioned to glory. I cannot fully describe what I felt at that moment. All I knew was that my prayer partner, my best friend, my secret keeper and shopping partner was no longer here with me. I just remember saying, "Now what am I going to do? Who will be there for me now?"I found my comfort in the word of God, **"When my mother and father forsake me, Then the Lord will take care of me."** My parents did not forsake me, but they were no longer here with me, and when I fully realized that at the grave, I was a complete wreck. "Both of you guys are gone! I still need you!" I made that declaration right there at my mom's burial.

My parents died seven years apart at the same age. I know right! Hence after that, I slipped into a little depression and was really sad. I hadn't shared with anyone at the time what I was feeling. While lying down one day, tears rolled down my face and the Lord said to me, "Either you are going to live or you are going to die." That was the moment I chose to live. But where do I start? How do I start? Those were the questions that were in my mind.

Sometimes things can happen to us, like the loss of a loved one, that can totally change the way we see life. For me, it was the loss of my parents. However, that may not be the same for you. It could be the ending of a bad relationship, a sickness, or even a divorce. I'm not sure what it is, but I am here to tell you that you can get through it. But you must be willing to be honest with yourself and those close to you. This is where you begin. I haven't always been the best communicator and my words did not always come out right. Yet, I am certain that if you are honest with yourself and God, His healing power can come in and heal those areas in your life that are keeping you stuck and in bondage. Freedom is a powerful thing. My pastor once said, "Healing is your responsibility." I thought it was so powerful! Sis, I don't know what caused or may be causing you to feel powerless, but it's time now to move forward. Let your pain push you to purpose.

Let's pray:

Heavenly Father,

I thank You for my sister who is reading this right now. Father, even in the midst of her pain, I pray that she would see You and help her to find purpose in her pain. Father, I pray that You would cause her to see that her affliction is just for a moment, but in fact you are working for us (her) a far more exceeding and eternal weight of glory (II Corinthians 4:17) In Jesus' Name, Amen.

I Choose to Live

Mental health matters and it's very important. A very close friend used to say that you need both the spiritual and natural. My first place to go is always prayer and anyone that knows me even a little bit knows that. Whether I am praying out loud, writing in my prayer journal or a prayer call, that is my initial destination. Prayer is very essential, and you won't ever hear me say otherwise. I have built my life on prayer, and it is my communication with the Lord. However, after my mom died, I realized that I had never even fully dealt with losing my dad, and I needed counseling. I didn't realize how it affected me naturally and mentally. Sometimes, when things happen to us, we put a Band-Aid on and just move on without fully dealing with the emotions of it all. Let's not forget about the not so good decision I spoke about earlier I made after losing my dad. We make impulsive decisions when we don't deal with the root of our problems.

The day I chose to live and not stay stuck anymore, I did not know who to call or where to begin. Google is a friend of mine; I just went on there and I looked up "Christian Counselors" and let the Lord do the rest. I called Refuge Christian Counseling because it was the name for me. **"God is our refuge and strength, a very present help in trouble."** Psalm 46:1 Their offices are closed now, but I remember when I walked into my initial consultation, I was so sad he thought I was going to need anti-depressants. We talked and he told me the price, and I felt the Lord leading and guiding, so I went back the following week with payment for at least a couple of months. I was ready to do the work.

I didn't share with anyone that I was going to counseling; that was something that I was doing for myself. Can I tell you that it was the best money I ever spent on myself? When you really decide that you want to be free and you don't want to stay in the same place that you are in, nothing will stop you, but you have to do the work. Your freedom won't just be handed to you; you have to go after it. It's a matter of choice. How bad do you want it? It is totally up to you. This may be hard. I thought it was hard too when my godsister, who is now a licensed life coach, said, "Stop all that crying and get back in this fight." Even if you have to cry, run or crawl all the way to the finish line, it's imperative that you get in this battle.

I read this, and it blessed me, and I pray it does the same for you: "I'm not telling you it's going to be easy, I'm telling you it's going to be worth it." Sis, I promise you it's all going to pay off. What they did may not have been your fault, what happened to you wasn't even your fault, I know you did not want them to go, but their time and purpose had been fulfilled. I know you feel like that relationship took everything that you had to give, and maybe you even feel like you won't love again. Yes, it did happen, and you may not ever get the apology that you are looking for.

Even in the loss of a loved one, you can't go back in time and say the things that you should have said when they were here, but God can and will give you peace in it all. Please know that your healing is your responsibility. The Bible says, **"And we know that God causes everything to work together for our good..." Romans 8:28.** Nothing that ever happens to us is for nothing. It has a purpose, find it and use it! Your testimony is going to save somebody's life. Come on sis, get up! Let's do this together!

Let's pray:

Heavenly Father,

Thank You that You gave us therapists and life coaches for help in sorting and dealing with the pressures of life. Lord, my healing and my freedom is my responsibility, so help me to go after it, knowing that You are right there by my side. In Jesus' Name, Amen

With Jesus, you will always win!

How Bad Do You Want It?

Listen, if you never think that you are good enough, you will never be good enough. If you never think that you are smart enough, you will never be smart enough. If you never think that you are pretty enough, no one else will either. If you think that you can't, then you won't. Why am I saying all of this? Because it is important that we align our thoughts and our words with what God says about us. How many opportunities have you missed out on simply because of the way you think or because of the words that have spoken in the atmosphere? I'm not really sure if you know this, but your words have power.

The Bible tells us that the power of life and death are in the tongue. We have to learn how to speak life into our dead situations. If we can conquer the battle in our mind, that's the battle. If I would have listened when the doctor told me that I would be putting myself in danger by getting pregnant, I would not have any more children. My two youngest children would not be here today. I know what they said but what did God say? If I had listened to my first boss who said, "This industry/career path is not for you, you need to find something else," I would have dropped out of property management a long time ago. I have been success-ful in this field for over ten plus years.

We have to learn how to combat the enemy's word with the word of God. He is and will always be on his job, so we must forever be on our job. If you never take the chance, you will always wonder. Growing up, I heard many times, "Nothing beats a failure but a try." Now that I am older, I understand that more than ever. If we look at it from a biblical standpoint the word says in James 2 :17 (NLT), " **So you see, faith by itself isn't good enough. Unless it produces good deeds, it is dead and useless.**" So, I ask, how bad do you really want it? I am not saying because I always got it right. I got it wrong on so many levels and I have had countless pity parties, but no one was showing up for the party. Don't waste any moments in your life, use them all. I promise the Lord is speaking even in those moments.

I was right in the middle of writing this book and my com-puter crashed. I mean it just stopped working. I tried to remain calm and not overreact, after all that was one thing that I used to do when things would not go as expected. Because this had happened before, I remained calm and tried to do what worked before, but it did not resolve my issue. I started to get a little concerned because if you know anything about a Macbook, they don't operate like a PC, so I was fresh out of ideas on what to do. By that time the tears began flowing. I could not understand why it was happening right in the middle of the book. I had fully committed myself to getting this book done, so why now? I could not even think. So, I phoned a friend at 4:52 am, so you know she is *really* a friend. She answered, "What's wrong?"She heard the whimper in my voice and I told her that my computer had stopped working. Her response was, "Do you have your oil?" I had already anointed my hands, but I went and put a little bit more on them. She continued, "We lay hands on the sick and they recover, so we're gonna lay hands on this computer and pray it will recover."

Let me just say this before I move on, the greatest friends are not necessarily the ones you can tell everything to or call every day. I mean they are good, but the greatest friends are the ones that will pray for you and completely come into agreement with the assignment on your life and speak life even when you can't. This is what she did. She prayed like this was her book and I mean she prayed, and we called on the name of the Lord. After the prayer, I was better and before I turned the computer on, we just sat and talked. Then I tried it again, and it still did not come on. At that point, I knew the Lord was speaking but I could not understand why this was happening. That's when I heard the Lord say, "Don't waste the assignment." My computer was supposed to stop me from writing that day, but I grabbed my phone, and I wrote about what happened.

I called my brother, and he heard the anguish in my voice. I told him, "I don't understand this. I told God I'm all in, so I don't understand why this is happening." He said this, "You trust God. Sometimes God has to stretch our faith to see if we are really committed." That's when the Lord brought back a word that He had spoken to me a week before. "Alisha, it's simple, how bad do you want it?" Is your yes just a yes when it's easy and when it is going the way you want it? Is your yes a yes only when it is easy, and you are not faced with any challenges? Or is your yes, a yes even when it's hard. We want everything easy and when it gets hard then we want to walk away. Will you complete the assignment even when it gets hard? There is someone reading this right now and God has given you an assignment, but you have faced so many obstacles that you have put it down and just walked away from it. It is time to pick it back up and get back to it. Stop overthinking it because overthinking is an enemy to us all. Overthinking will have you stuck. Don't be so focused on the method that God is using that you skip over the process, and you miss the lesson and the blessing.

Did you really think that the enemy would not try to stop the plan of God for your life? Did you really think that he would let it go on without a hinge of trouble? I will be honest and tell you that I had that premature thought, and I quickly got my life together and now I am telling you to do the same thing. Don' t waste it, use it. It's not for you, it's for someone else and their deliverance is contingent on you completing the assignment. Yes, I said it! Somebody is waiting on you. They need to hear your testimony, they need to hear your story of deliverance, they need to know that "with God all things are possible." They need to know that if He did it for you, He can certainly do it for them! I just need you to get back in the fight.

Fight with tears in your eyes, fight with your limp, just keep walking. While you are walking it out, God is working it out. Even if you can't walk and you need to crawl, just get there. You must remember it's not a "you" thing, it's a "God" thing. You might be nervous, but be nervous *and* determined. Let your nervousness make you seek the face of God.

Let's pray:

Heavenly Father,

I pray for my friend who is reading this right now. Father, I pray that she will not give up on the assignment that you have given her to do. Father, I thank You that she was created in You for good works. I thank You that Your promises are yes and amen, and every promise spoken over her life will come to pass. In Jesus' Name, Amen.

You got this!

Be Authentic

Learn how to surround yourself with people that want to see you win. So many times we attach ourselves to people that are not adding to our lives, but in fact subtracting and draining us for the sake of calling them friends. Proverbs 17:17(a), "**A friend loves at all times...**" This scripture by itself is so powerful and speaks volumes to the one we decide to call friends. I don't think I have ever looked up the definition of what a friend really is, so I decided to look it up and there were two definitions that were magnified to me. The first one was *one who is not an enemy and who is on the side*. When I read this, I wondered, are they really on your side or are they an undercover enemy? I can't answer that, only you can.

The second definition really hit home for me in a personal way. *A person who acts as a supporter*. I had a friend who shared with me how I made them feel. I will be honest when I was listening to them speak and the tears just began to fall, I was unaware of how I made them feel and it hurt me to know this. I apologized profusely, and I was forgiven, but I changed my prayers directly after. I asked God to help me to be a better friend.

Why did I choose to share this? First, we don't realize how our actions may affect others and so every so often we need to do a friend check. Ask yourself, am I being a good friend or am I in this friendship just for what I can gain? If you can't answer these questions, then you need to check your friendships. The other reason I chose to share this is because I have enough bad friendships to know that when God blesses you with genuine people, you learn to appreciate them. The Bible tells us in Romans 12:10 to **"be devoted to one another with (authentic) brotherly affection"** It's the word *authentic* for me. The only way to be real with others is to be real with ourselves. Part of me seeing myself through God's eyes was seeing the parts that God needed to do a work on. I allowed Him to show where I was not honoring him. My prayer for you is that you be authentic in your friendships with others but most importantly with Jesus Christ. John 15:13 declares, **"... Greater love has no one than this: to lay down one's life for one's friends."** Jesus is the ultimate friend.

Let's pray:

Heavenly Father,

I thank You so much that You show us when we are in godly and ungodly friendships. God help us to be godly friends to the people that You have placed in our lives. Help us to honor You with our friendships. In Jesus' Name, Amen.

Fully Committed

It took me a long time to see myself the way God sees me and to fully come into agreement with the plans that He had for my life. It did not happen for me overnight. Sometimes God must bring us back to a childlike faith. When children approach their parents for something that they want, they are not concerned with what, when or how, they just believe that it's going to happen. Even if it takes a long time, they don't give up, they come back and ask if not everyday, every other day. My point is that they believe they are going to get what they have requested. Sometimes God must bring us back to the basics. My basics may not be your basics. But for me, God had to bring me back to a place where I was completely relying on him. He had to bring me back to a place where I believed again. It does not matter how many people see, speak or tell you about what God has for you, if you don't see or believe for yourself then you will remain in a place of bondage.

The Lord gave me this assignment about five years ago. After I completed therapy, I created a vision board in 2016. The Lord spoke to me clearly about what He wanted and what He wanted me to do. I wrote it down and then I made some notes in my phone, but that's all I did. I believed God for everything except for what He told me to do because I was not confident in my abilities to complete the task. Let me pause right here. Did you know you can talk yourself out of your own blessings? You can talk yourself out of the place that God intended you to be because of the way that you feel about yourself. The Bible tells us in Psalms 139:14, **"We are fearfully and wonderfully made."** But what happens when we don't believe what God says about us? Do we forfeit the promises spoken over our lives? Does God remove His hand from us? The answer is no. God is forever present in our lives, even when we can't feel Him. God is always there, He never left. He was, and is, just waiting on you to see yourself the way He sees you.

I had to learn the same thing that you must learn and that is to remove all the lies that the enemy has told you. I learned to remove, replace and repeat in church. Remove the idea that it's too late because the Bible says in Philippians 1:6, **"Being confident of this very thing, that he who has begun a good work in you will complete it."** Remove the idea that it's not possible because the Bible says in Luke 18:27, **"With man it is impossible, but with God all things are possible."** I hear you saying, but what about this mountain that is standing in front of me. Well, the Bible says in Matthew 17:20 (NLT), **"I tell you the truth, if you had faith even as a mustard seed, you could say to this mountain, Move from here to there, and it would move..."** I hear you, does God love me even after everything that I have done? Yes, He does. You know how I know? Because the Bible says, **"Nothing can**

separate you/me from the Love of Christ." You repeat all these truths to yourselves until you start to believe them and then do what I did, put one foot in front of the other and move forward.

There is nothing that you have done that God cannot not use. It is all a part of the plan. So here I am almost six years later, and the dream is finally coming to pass. It does not matter how long it takes as long as you get it done. When you give God your yes, I don't want you to think that you won't be met with any obstacles. Because now the enemy is mad, his goal was to stop you, make you put the pen down, not start the business, or keep you in a place of brokenness. Yet, because you decided to keep going, you must be on your job with prayer, fasting, and reading the word of God. When the enemy intensifies his attack, you intensify your praise and your worship. You stay on your post and don't you come down!

How committed are you to getting it done? I had to ask myself that question along this journey. Sometimes we can say with our mouth that we are committed but then our actions prove differently. I was sitting on the side of my bed one morning that I did not write. I just wanted to hear God, and I had been asking the Lord about a decision I was contemplating. It would not have taken me from my writing, but it would have been a major distraction that I could not afford. God had finally given me His stamp of approval and pushed me forward. But I had to decide. The Lord said to me at that moment, "Alisha it's really simple, you need to make a choice." That was the moment that

I chose Him and decided to fully commit to the assignment of finishing my book.

I began to weep before the Lord. I had finally made the decision to make God first in my life. I am not saying that God was never first, but I think that we are all guilty of saying *yes* to God and then letting the trials of life cause us to drop our assignment. I asked a question at the beginning because when we set out to complete the task, we are ready and excited! We are looking ahead before we complete the work, making plans and so on. However, at the first sign of trouble, we want to stop and give up in the process. The negative thoughts start coming and then before we know it, we just stop. I am saying this because this is what I would do every time, but this time was different. I wanted this not for anyone else but for myself, and I wanted to steward it well.

When you fully commit to Christ and what He has for you and you give your plans to Him, you are committing Calvary. When Jesus committed to His assignment, He committed to Judas, He committed to the Garden of Gethsemane, He committed to being rejected by Peter, and in all of this, He completed His assignment. So, I ask you, how bad do you really want it? Don't let the appearance of the assignment in the natural trip you up; you must look beyond what you see in the natural and see it spiritually. Jesus said, **"O My Father, if it is possible, let this cup pass from Me**; then He says, in that same verse, **"nevertheless, not as I will, but as you will."** You need a nevertheless spirit in you that says, "I'm not giving up and I am not giving in". Anything worth having, you will have to work for it. It will not be handed to you, you will have to sacrifice for it. You may even have to cut away some things and even some people, but the choice is yours. You must decide. The Bible says, **"Commit your way to the Lord; Trust in Him also and He will do it."** Psalm 37:5. It does not get any simpler than that.

The Bible gives us what we need to do to get it done. Stop looking at how, stop wondering who God is going to send, stop saying I will wait till I get myself together so I can fully commit, stop saying I don't have time. These are all excuses and time waits for no one and procrastination is an enemy to us all. You have what it takes. Go back and take "it," whatever your it is, off the shelf and get back to work. The senior saints would say, "there is no time like the present."

My prayer for you is that you would be committed, not just to the outcome but to the process. You don't want to skip over the process because as the mother in church would say, "It's for your learning." The process is where you are being developed and shaped. There are some lessons which are necessary to complete the assignment. The real flex is not trying to explain why you are doing what you are doing, not trying to explain why you are where you are, or why you had to make some changes. Instead, you are just committed to what the Lord has for you in this season of your life. You can't explain faith moves.

Let's pray:

Heavenly Father,

I thank You for my sister who is reading this right now. I pray right now that she will be committed to You and the plans that You have for them. Father, I pray Jeremiah 29:11 over her. For I know the plans and thoughts that I have for you, says the Lord, plans for peace and well-being and not for disaster, to give you a future and a hope. In Jesus' Name, Amen.

Stay Committed!

You Were Created For It

I have shared with you some of the most intimate parts of me and my prayer is that you will be helped and be able to move forward in everything that God has called you to be. I did not do everything right; I did not dot every "i" and cross every "t." Listen, I did not always have the best communication skills, as I stated earlier, I ran from my calling many years before I said *yes* to God. If I am honest, there are still days where I want to take back my *yes*. However, the Bible says, **"In his kindness God called you to share in his eternal glory by means of Christ Jesus. So after you have suffered for a little while, HE will restore, support and strengthen you, and he will place you on a firm foundation."** 1 Peter 5:10 (nlt)

While I was writing this, my spirit got happy. God is the only one who confirms and validates who you are, and He will place you where you are supposed to be. You are not who they said you were. So, they left you. The sickness is not unto death. I know it happened but it's just a part of your story. I used to sing a song in church entitled, "The Best of My Story." Can I tell you that the best part of your story has yet to be told? This is only the beginning; you have not seen your best days yet. Stop allowing people to present you with anything. The enemy has a way of dressing himself up in exactly what you are looking for. Don't just look at the wrapping, but look on the inside. This goes not just for people but for every area of your life. Don't settle, be willing to wait on the Lord. He does all things well.

So, they rejected you. Rejection sometimes points you in a better direction. God still has a plan and a purpose. Don't focus so much on what was and how many times you may think that you got it wrong, just learn the lesson. God may change the route, but your destination will remain the same, just ask the children of Israel. My pastor once preached a sermon entitled "Welcome to the Wilderness." It was a great sermon, but one of the things that was magnified to me was when he talked about our mind-sets. Sometimes we can't go the route as planned because God must break some strongholds off our minds. It is not God's will that we stay stuck and not fulfill our purpose. This may sound crazy, but when it's my time to go be with the Lord, I want to leave empty, assignment completed, nothing left undone.

When you are in a season of transition, it can seem like it's one of the hardest places because God is moving you to another level; don't fight it, just move with it. This season of transition is your preparation time. So don't cry about your prep time, because God is getting you ready for prime time. In my season of transition, someone sent this scripture to me, and it blessed me, so now I am giving it to you in hopes that it blesses you as well. **Genesis 41:52: "He named his second (son) Ephraim (fruitfulness) for "God has caused me to be fruitful and very successful in the land of my suffering."** I had to read that scripture several times before it took root in my spirit, then after I allowed it into my spirit, I began to blossom.

You were created for a purpose. You were created to bring glory to God in your life. You were not created to fit in. I struggled with this for a long time because for so long, I wanted just to fit in. But the Lord said this to me, and I am saying it to you: "You were not created to fit in or to be a part of the crowd, but you were in fact created to stand out. Embrace it and walk it out. Don't worry about trying to conform to the world standards, I did not make you that way." The word of God says, **"and be not conformed to this world."** You don't have to be like others to fit in. There are select people that God has ordained to help you walk out your purpose. So be the best version of you and in being that best version, you will be authentic. **"For we are his workmanship, created in Christ Jesus for good works, which God prepared beforehand that we should walk in them." Ephesians 2:10** What you are carrying is much larger than what you could even imagine. You have what it takes to get the job done. I believe in you!

Let's pray:

Heavenly Father,

I thank You for the opportunity to write this book and share parts of my life. Father, I pray for my friend reading this book right now. I pray that she will know that all things are possible with You" I thank You for giving her everything she needs to complete the assignment. In Jesus' Name, Amen.

You are still called, you are still chosen, you are still anointed. Your gifts and callings are not predicated on where you were but on who you are and whose you are! You are amazing because God made you that way!

About the Author

B orn and raised in the city of Chicago, Alisha D. Johnson uses her voice in a multitude of ways to inspire the masses.

Answering the call to ministry, Alisha preached her first sermon on January 18, 2015.

As a psalmist of the Lord, she has previously served in several musical capacities such as minister of music for over ten years and as director of one of the largest youth choirs in the midwest. Alisha has also faithfully shared her gift of song with many community choirs throughout the city of Chicago, including Walt Whtman and The Soul Children of Chicago.

By day, Alisha is employed as a property manager in Chicago. After hours, she is committed to sharing more of her story through speaking opportunities and, in the future, writing more books.

Alisha proudly wears the titles of daughter, sister, friend and servant, but one of her most beloved names is mom, given by her four beautiful children.